5.4
livar
mous

FAMOUS NAVY ATTACK PLANES

GEORGE SULLIVAN

DODD, MEAD & COMPANY
New York

Copyright © 1986 by George Sullivan
All rights reserved
No part of this book may be reproduced in any form
without permission in writing from the publisher
Distributed in Canada by
McClelland and Stewart Limited, Toronto
Manufactured in the United States of America

1 2 3 4 5 6 7 8 9 10

Library of Congress Cataloging-in-Publication Data

Sullivan, George, 1927–
    Famous navy attack planes.

    Summary: Traces the development of Navy aviation by
examining specific types of planes, primarily attack
planes and bombers, from before World War I to recent
times.
    1. Attack planes—United States—History—Juvenile
literature. 2. Bombers—United States—History—
Juvenile literature. 3. Reconnaissance aircraft—United
States—History—Juvenile literature. 4. United States.
Navy—Aviation—History—Juvenile literature.
5. Aeronautics, Military—United States—History—
Juvenile literature. [1. Attack planes—History.
2. Bombers—History. 3. Airplanes—History. 4. United
States. Navy—Aviation—History] I. Title.
UG1242.A28S86   1986   358.4′2   86-6201
ISBN 0-396-08770-1

INTRODUCTION

Naval aviation had its beginnings on November 14, 1910. That day, Eugene Ely, a 24-year-old test pilot for the Curtiss Aeroplane and Motor Company, guided a fragile-looking biplane into the air from a wooden ramp that had been laid down on the foredeck of the light cruiser USS *Birmingham* that was anchored off Norfolk, Virginia.

At the end of the ramp, the plane dipped scarily, then rolled to one side, a wheel skimming the water's surface. But Ely managed to keep the plane in the air, gain some altitude, and land on a sandy strip of beach some 2½ miles to the west.

In January of the next year, Ely landed a Curtiss aircraft on a platform that had been built on the deck of the cruiser USS *Pennsylvania* in San Francisco Bay. An ingenious braking system was used. As Ely eased the plane down toward the ramp, three hooks dangling from between the aircraft's wheels snagged taut ropes that had been strung across the width of the deck.

Each rope was tied to a 50-pound sandbag at either end. The weight of the sandbags braked the plane's forward speed before it reached the end of the ramp.

The next day, San Francisco newspapers hailed the feat with such headlines as: AIR MONSTER SWOOPS TO WARSHIP'S DECK and ELY MAKES NAVAL HISTORY.

From a technical standpoint, Ely's flights did not accomplish a great deal (although the principle of the cable arrester system that had been used to brake Ely's plane has remained in use to this day). But they did clearly demonstrate that the airplane could be at home at sea.

Today, the U.S. Navy operates one of the biggest air arms in the world. With 5,500 aircraft, it is bigger than the air forces of all but three countries—the United States, the Soviet Union, and the Republic of China.

This book and its companion volume, *Famous Navy Fighter Planes*, describe and picture the most significant aircraft in the growth and development of American naval aviation.

The constant struggle was for safer, faster, and more powerful flying machines. Each of the planes examined here contributed toward achieving that goal.

The author is grateful to many individuals who helped him in the preparation of this book. Special thanks are due Lt. J. A. Kendrick, Anna C. Urband, Bob Carlisle, David Kronberger, Office of Information, U.S. Navy; Roy Grossnick, Gwendolyn Rich, John Elliott, Aviation History Office, Office of the Chief of Naval Operations; Phil Edwards, Norman Richards, National Air and Space Museum; Capt. Leighton W. Smith, Jr., USS *America*; Grover Walker, Naval Aviation Museum, Pensacola, Florida; Barbara Weiner, USS *Intrepid* Sea-Air-Space Museum; Jerry Borenstein, Naval Aviation Commandery; Ira Chart, Northrop; R. F. Foster, McDonnell; J. F. Isabel, General Dynamics; Francene Crum, Martin Marietta; Francesca Kurti, TLC Custom Labs; and Rear Adm. (Ret.) John J. Schieffelin.

CONTENTS

Curtiss A-1 Triad resting on its float in shallow water.

CURTISS A-1 TRIAD

Glenn Curtiss, a motorcycle manufacturer from Hammondsport, New York, was the first American to fly after the Wright Brothers. Like the Wrights, Curtiss designed and built his own airplanes.

On November 14, 1910, Curtiss pilot Eugene Ely made aviation history when he flew one of his employer's aircraft from the long ramp that had been laid down on the deck of the cruiser *Birmingham* (page 3). Ely later landed the Curtiss plane on a similar ramp aboard the battleship *Pennsylvania*.

Between the years 1911 and 1913, Curtiss supplied the Navy with its first airplanes. The very first, designated the A-1, was a hydro-aeroplane (as it was called in those days), a flying boat.

Not only could the aircraft land and take off from the water with floats, it could also be equipped with wheels for land operation. And when fitted with both wheels and floats, the plane could land in offshore waters and taxi onto the beach. Because it could be operated in three different ways, the plane was called the Triad.

The Triad was first flown by Curtiss himself at

Hammondsport, New York, on July 1, 1911. Later flights were made by Lt. T. G. Ellyson, the first Navy pilot.

The first engine with which the Triad was fitted was rated at 50 hp. Later, with a 75-hp engine, the aircraft reached an altitude of nearly 1,000 feet. The Triad had a range of about 60 miles.

Through 1911 and much of 1912, the Triad was used by the Navy for experimental flying in Chesapeake Bay. The plane registered a number of historic achievements. Once, with Lt. Ellyson at the controls and Lt. John H. Towers as a passenger, the Triad flew from Annapolis, Maryland, to Milford Haven, Virginia, a distance of 112 miles, in 122 minutes. The aircraft set an altitude record of 900 feet on June 12, 1912.

Curtiss delivered a plane designated the A-2 to the Navy on July 13, 1911. In October of the following year, the A-2 remained aloft for 6 hours, 10 minutes, a remarkable feat.

The next Navy airplanes, the A-3 and A-4, were also built by Curtiss. The A-3 set an American altitude record of 6,300 feet.

As for the A-1, it made a total of 285 flights. It was damaged and repaired many times. A crash at Annapolis in October, 1912, ended the Triad's historic career.

Other Data (Model: A-1)
Wingspan: 32 ft.
Length: 28 ft., 7 in.
Power Plant: 75-hp water-cooled Curtiss V-8
Loaded Weight: 1,575 lb.
Maximum Speed: 60 mph.

Triad is hoisted aboard USS *Pennsylvania* in February, 1911.

CURTISS H-16

During World War I, in which the United States became a combatant in 1917, the Navy's flying corps was chiefly active in antisubmarine patrols. By the time the war ended in 1918, Navy and Marine Corps pilots had attacked twenty-five submarines, sinking or heavily damaging a dozen of them.

The plane that carried out these sorties was a giant flying boat, the Curtiss H-16. Officially designated a patrol/bomber flying boat, the aircraft was armed with as many as six .30-caliber machine guns and carried four 230-pound bombs. It was operated by a four-man crew.

The H-16 had its beginnings in 1914 when an American aviation enthusiast named Lewis Rodman Wanamaker placed an order with Curtiss to build a huge flying boat which he planned to use for a transatlantic flight. When the war broke out, Wanamaker had to shelve his plans.

The plane, which had been named the *America*, was sold to Great Britain's Royal Naval Air Service. The Royal Navy soon found the aircraft to be just what was needed in protecting ships in convoy from submarine attack. More were ordered from Curtiss.

In 1916, the U.S. Navy ordered an improved version of the plane, designating it the H-12. The aircraft featured longer wings and a more powerful engine. When H-12s were sold to Britain, they were called *Large Americas*.

More improvements in the plane resulted in the H-16, introduced in 1917. Since Curtiss could not meet the demand for the plane, the Navy began manufacturing H-16s at the Naval Aircraft Factory in Philadelphia. The first H-16 to be built there was completed on March 27, 1918.

In total, the Navy built 150 H-16s. Curtiss turned out 124. They operated from twelve different bases along the Atlantic seaboard and from two bases in Canada and one in the Canal Zone. H-16 bases were also established in France, England, Ireland, Italy, and the Azores.

The big Curtiss flying boats represented naval aviation's major contribution during World War I.

Other Data (Model: H-16)
Wingspan: 95 ft., 1 in.
Length: 46 ft., 1½ in.
Power Plant: Two 40-hp Liberties
Loaded Weight: 10,900 lb.
Maximum Speed: 95 mph at sea level

H-16s played an important role in World War I. Here a pair of the giant flying boats is pictured near Pensacola, Florida, in 1919.

Like other early Navy aircraft, the DT was equipped with floats to operate as a seaplane.

DOUGLAS DT

The value of the bomber as a weapon of war was clearly demonstrated in the summer of 1921 by Brig. Gen. William "Billy" Mitchell of the Army Air Corps. In tests conducted off the Virginia capes, Mitchell's rickety little bombing planes quickly destroyed and sank a German cruiser and battleship, ships that had been surrendered to the Allies during World War I.

Navy pilots of the day were not impressed with the tests, however. They realized that under actual warfare conditions enemy vessels would not be sitting ducks. Not only would they be underway, perhaps even zigzagging, they would defend themselves with antiaircraft fire.

Since high-level bombing would never accomplish much, aviation experts figured the Navy would have to attack from above with dive bombers and torpedo bombers.

The torpedo bomber, after an approach that took it low along the surface, dropped its torpedo into the water. A self-contained propulsion system then drove the torpedo to its target.

The Douglas DT was one of the Navy's first successful torpedo bombers. It was also the first military airplane produced by the Douglas Aircraft Company (the McDonnell-Douglas Company today).

A chunky little single-seat biplane, the DT was designed under the supervision of Donald W. Douglas himself. It had wings that could be folded to store the plane, and operated with wheels or a pair of floats. It could also carry a 1,835-pound torpedo under its fuselage. The Navy ordered three DT-1s in 1921.

The plane proved to be a big success. Douglas continued to modify the aircraft, however, making it a two-seater, with one seat behind the other. An observer went along in the second seat.

The Navy purchased 38 DT-2s, as this version was called. By 1925, DT-1s and DT-2s were in service at all major Navy bases in the United States.

The same year, the Navy began experimenting with catapult launches from the flight deck of the USS *Langley*. On these, a plane would be hurled into the air by means of a device resembling a steam-powered slingshot. The DT was the plane chosen for the test.

While the DT was meant primarily as a torpedo bomber, it also saw service in scouting, observation, and in aerial gunnery practice.

Other Data (Model: D-2)
Wingspan: 50 ft.
Length: 37 ft., 7½ in.
Power Plant: One 400-hp Liberty
Loaded Weight: 7,923 lb.
Maximum Speed: 99 mph at sea level

A Douglas DT-2 lifts into the air from the flight deck of the carrier *Langley*.

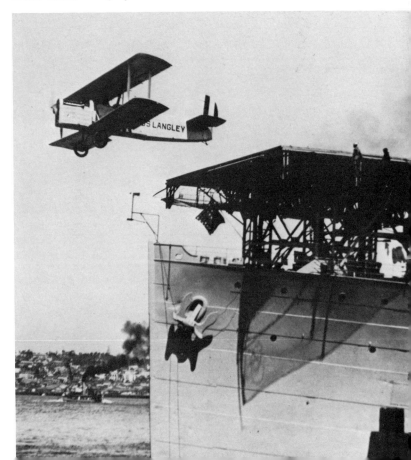

Curtiss CS had three uses: bombing, scouting, and torpedo launching.

CURTISS CS, MARTIN SC

Designed for scouting, bombing, and torpedo launching, the Curtiss CS-1 made its appearance at the end of 1923. A large biplane, it was unusual in that its lower wing had a greater span than its upper wing. (Wings were usually the same size, but if they were of different sizes, it was standard for the upper wing to be the longer.)

The CS-1 was also somewhat out of the ordinary because it was a three-seater. There were accommodations for a pilot, a gunner, and a torpedo man.

The torpedo itself was carried under the fuselage. Curtiss designed the plane with an interchangeable float wheel or float system.

The CS-1 was equipped with a 525-hp Wright T-2 water-cooled inline engine. (An inline engine is one in which the cylinders are arranged in a straight line, rather than in a circular, H or V pattern.)

Six CS-1s was ordered by the Navy. An improved model of the aircraft, boasting a 575-hp Wright T-3, was designated the CS-2. The Navy bought two of these.

When the Navy sought additional planes, Curtiss lost out in the bidding to the Glenn L. Martin Co. Martin produced 35 aircraft of the CS-1 design, but called them SC-1s. They went into service in 1925.

Martin also built 40 CS-2s, designating them SC-2s. These were delivered by the end of 1925.

The SCs (or CSs) were capable performers. They could operate at altitudes of up to 8,000 feet and had a range of just over one thousand miles. Nevertheless, they did not remain in service very long. Indeed, by 1927 almost all versions of the plane had been withdrawn from active duty.

Other Data (Model: SC-2)
Wingspan: 56 ft., 7 in.
Length: 37 ft., 8¾ in.
Power Plant: One 585-hp Wright T-3
Loaded Weight: 8,422 lb.
Maximum Speed: 103 mph at sea level

A three-seat aircraft, the Curtiss CS was unusual in that it had a lower wing that was longer than the upper wing.

CURTISS F8C HELLDIVER

Several times early in this century, U.S. Marines occupied Nicaragua. During one such occupation in 1928, a small group of marines became isolated and surrounded by a bandit group.

Other marines directed marine pilots, flying Curtiss F8C Falcons, to bomb the outlaw band. The two opposing forces were so close together that precision bombing was necessary. The pilots took their planes high into the sky, then dove straight down, putting the 500-pound bombs on the enemy strongpoints without endangering their comrades.

The F8C Falcon was meant to be an all-purpose aircraft. It was designed as a two-seat fighter that could also operate as a light bomber and observation plane.

But following the success of the marine operation in Nicaragua, the aircraft was modified to make dive bombing its principal function.

The main change was from a water-cooled Wright engine to an air-cooled Pratt & Whitney Wasp. The plane's two .30-caliber machine guns were moved from the lower to the upper wing. The

Helldiver could carry a 500-pound bomb beneath its fuselage, or four 116-pound bombs under the wings.

CURTISS
F8C1 A-7945
LIGHT BOMBER
THREE QUARTER
FRONT VIEW

Helldiver was powered by a 450-hp air-cooled Pratt & Whitney Wasp engine.

aircraft, which could carry a single 500-pound bomb under the fuselage or four 116-pound bombs in racks under the wings, was given a new name—Helldiver.

With the F8C, the Navy carried out a decision to include two-seat aircraft in its mix of carrier planes. The additional crew member could help to navigate and communicate. He could also relieve the pilot at the controls and, thus, the range of the plane could be increased.

News of the dive-bombing F8C reached Japanese and German plane-makers, and they began developing dive bombers of their own. These planes would emerge as one of the most frightening weapons of World War II.

Despite its significance, the F8C Helldiver was not a notable airplane from a technical standpoint. It was relatively slow and not very maneuverable. What it did have was wings so strong that it could endure the steepest dives without fear of structural failure.

Other Data (Model: F8C-5)
Wingspan: 32 ft.
Length: 25 ft., 8 in.
Power Plant: One 450-hp Pratt & Whitney Wasp
Loaded Weight: 4,020 lb.
Maximum Speed: 146 mph at sea level

A two-seater with a metal-covered fuselage and fabric-covered wings, the BM was designed as a dive bomber.

MARTIN BM

In 1928, the Bureau of Aeronautics called for the development of a special-purpose dive bomber. The plane had to be capable of pulling out of a high-speed vertical dive from 6,000 feet while carrying a 1,000-pound bomb or torpedo beneath its fuselage.

The specifications ordered that the plane was to be metal-framed and with a metal-covered fuselage and tail. The wings were to be fabric-covered.

The plane was to be a two-seater, the pilot in front, a gunner behind.

Prototypes for the new plane were ordered from the Naval Aircraft Factory in Philadelphia and the Glenn L. Martin Co., then located in Baltimore. The prototypes were delivered to the Anacostia Naval Air Station in Washington, D.C., in 1930 for testing.

Once it was demonstrated that the airplane was capable of pulling out of the steepest possible dives with a full bombload, the Navy began ordering the craft. It was designated the BM-1, a new bomber category.

Deliveries of the first twelve planes ordered by the Navy began in September, 1931. A slightly improved version of the aircraft, called the BM-2, was later developed. The Navy ordered sixteen BM-2s.

BMs could climb to an altitude of 10,000 feet in ten minutes. They could operate at 18,000 feet. Their cruising speed was 120 mph.

Although the BMs were designed primarily as dive bombers, they first saw service as torpedo bombers aboard the carrier *Lexington*. Other BMs were assigned to the *Langley*.

The BMs continued to serve with the fleet until 1937. After that, they were used as utility planes at shore bases. The last of the BMs was scrapped in 1940.

Other Data (Model: BM-2)
Wingspan: 41 ft.
Length: 28 ft., 9 in.
Power Plant: One 625-hp Pratt & Whitney Hornet
Loaded Weight: 6,218 lb.
Maximum Speed: 146 mph at 6,000 ft.

The BM also served as a torpedo bomber. Here, carrying a torpedo, aircraft takes off from the carrier *Lexington*.

GREAT LAKES BG-1

A two-seat dive bomber that had the ability to carry a 1,000-pound bomb beneath its fuselage, the BG-1 was the only airplane produced for the U.S. Navy by the Great Lakes Aircraft Corporation of Cleveland, Ohio, in the eight years the firm was in operation.

The contract for the plane was issued on June 13, 1932. An experimental version of the aircraft was ready for flight tests in mid-1933. In November of that year, after the testing had proved successful, the BG-1 went into production.

The first planes went on active duty in October, 1934. They were assigned to the aircraft carrier *Ranger*.

The BG-1 was armed with two .30-caliber machine guns. One gun fired forward, the other aft.

The aircraft's 750-hp Pratt & Whitney Twin Wasp Junior was of radial design, that is, its cylinders were arranged around the crankshaft in a circular pattern.

This engine made the BG-1 one of the most powerful of the Navy's early bombers. The aircraft could climb to an altitude of 5,000 feet in about 5½ minutes, which was regarded as outstanding by standards of the day. The plane's maximum speed was 189 mph, also excellent. The BG-1 had a range of 548 miles while toting its 1,000-pound payload.

The Great Lakes Aircraft Corporation went out of business in 1936. By that time, it had supplied the Navy with 60 BG-1s. Of that number, about half went to Marine Corps units.

With the Navy, the BG-1 saw service with only one squadron. These planes remained in service until 1938.

The BG-1 continued to serve in a utility role at shore bases for several more years, however. Right up until 1940, in fact, a Marine unit in Quantico, Virginia, flew BG-1s.

Other Data (Model: BG-1)
Wingspan: 36 ft.
Length: 28 ft., 9 in.
Power Plant: One 750-hp Pratt & Whitney Twin Wasp Junior
Loaded Weight: 6,347 lb.
Maximum Speed: 189 mph at 8,900 ft.

The two-seat Great Lakes BG-1 was capable of carrying a 1,000-pound bombload.

CURTISS SBC HELLDIVER

The last combat biplane ever produced in the United States, the Curtiss SBC Helldiver began life as a monoplane. First flown in 1933, it was, in fact, a parasol monoplane, a monoplane in which the wing was mounted above the fuselage. This design was intended to improve the pilot's range of vision during carrier takeoffs and landings.

During flight tests, however, the single wing proved unstable for the dive-bombing role the aircraft was meant to play. Another prototype was ordered. A wholly new airplane, a biplane, was the result. This aircraft made its first flight on December 9, 1935.

Still not completely satisfied, the Navy ordered that the plane's 625-hp Wright Whirlwind engine be replaced with a 750-hp Pratt & Whitney Wasp.

That did the trick. In August, 1936, the Navy began ordering the plane, which by now was designated the SBC-3. The first order called for 83 planes.

More improvements followed. For the SBC-4, a still more powerful engine was ordered, a 950-hp Wright Cyclone. This gave the aircraft a cruising speed of 127 mph and a maximum speed of 237 mph. It could climb at the rate of 1,860 feet per minute. The SBC-4 carried a 1,000-pound bomb.

A total of 174 SBC-4s were ordered by the Navy. In March, 1939, when the first of these planes be-

In the early design stage, the SBC Helldiver was a parasol-wing monoplane.

When the single-wing version was found to be unstable, the SBC was redesigned as a biplane.

gan coming off the production line, war clouds were gathering. World War II in Europe began later that year with Germany's invasion of Poland. The Navy sent 50 of its SBC-4s to France to aid in the defense of that country.

But France fell to the Germans before the planes could be delivered and they were taken over by the British. Since the distance the plane required to take off was too great for British aircraft carriers, these planes had to be assigned to shore stations.

Most SBC-4s went to equip Navy and Marine scouting and bombing carrier squadrons. When the Japanese attacked Pearl Harbor on December 7, 1941, the Navy had about 200 SBCs in operation aboard carriers.

By that time, however, the plane was outdated. As quickly as possible, the SBC was replaced by the faster, more powerful Douglas SBD Dauntless.

Other Data (Model: SBC-4)
Type: Carrier-based scout bomber
Wingspan: 34 ft.
Length: 28 ft., 4 in.
Power Plant: One 950-hp Wright Cyclone 9
Loaded Weight: 7,632 lb.
Maximum Speed: 237 mph at 15,200 ft.

A total of 3,290 PBY Catalinas were built, making it the most-produced flying boat in history.

CONSOLIDATED PBY CATALINA

During World War II, the Japanese captured two tiny pieces of the Territory of Alaska. (Alaska did not become a state until 1959.) The American soil in question consisted of Attu and Kiska, two cold, fog-shrouded, and largely uninhabited Aleutian Islands south and west of the Alaskan mainland.

On June 10, 1942, the Japanese forces that had secretly occupied the islands were discovered by a PBY Catalina patrol bomber. The next day, PBYs operating from Atka Island, more than 300 miles to the east, began bombing Japanese positions on Attu and Kiska.

The PBYs were well suited for the struggle to retake the islands. They continued to fly long distances to bomb Japanese installations. They sank enemy submarines and battled Japanese fighter planes. They also ferried troops and supplies. After the American forces had retaken the islands in 1943, Catalinas were singled out for special praise.

The prototype for the PBY Catalina was built in the Buffalo, New York, plant of the Consolidated Aircraft Corporation. It was designed as a high-wing monoplane with its wings and two engines above the hull. It carried a crew of six.

The prototype made its first flight on March 28, 1935. The Navy ordered 60 Catalinas in the fall of 1935.

In the years that followed, the Navy ordered hundreds of additional PBYs. Thus, when the

United States entered World War II in December, 1941, the Catalina was on active duty with the Navy in almost every part of the world.

In the first year of the war in the Pacific, the PBY Catalina, with a range of 2,110 miles, and the Air Force's Boeing B-17 Flying Fortress were the only two aircraft available capable of flying long distances. As a result, PBYs were used not only as bombers, but in every other possible role. The Catalina won a reputation for reliability that few aircraft have ever matched.

A total of 3,290 Catalinas were built, making it the most-produced flying boat in aviation history.

Some PBYs remained in service for years after World War II, even into the late 1960s. These aircraft were used mainly in air-sea rescue missions.

Other Data (Model: PBY-5)
Wingspan: 104 ft.
Length: 63 ft., 10 in.
Power Plant: Two 1,200-hp Pratt & Whitney
   Twin Wasp radial piston engines
Loaded Weight: 34,000 lb.
Maximum Speed: 189 mph

Production of the Catalina ended after World War II. But the aircraft remained in use for many years, flying air-sea rescue missions.

CURTISS BFC GOSHAWK

The first planes in the BFC Goshawk line were fighter planes. But at about the time they began rolling off the production line, the Navy decided that all of its fighters should also be capable of delivering bombs. The BFC Goshawk became a bomber-fighter. That's what "BF" stands for; the "C" is for Curtiss, the plane's manufacturer.

The Goshawk (the name refers to a large and powerful hawk, with broad and rounded wings) had its beginnings in the early 1930s when the Navy called upon Curtiss to design a single-seat fighter with better performance qualities than the fighters then in service.

Curtiss developed not one, but two prototypes. One was powered by a 600-hp Wright Whirlwind engine with a three-blade propeller. The other prototype was fitted with a 700-hp Wright Cyclone and a two-blade prop. The prototype with the less powerful engine was the Navy's choice. The first production models were delivered in 1932.

With its open cockpit and clean and angular lines, the Goshawk was one of the most eye-appealing biplanes ever built. It was a favorite of model builders for almost half a century.

A handsome plane with clean lines, the BFC Goshawk was a favorite with model builders.

Later versions of the Goshawk were fitted with a retractable landing gear that the pilot operated with a hand crank.

The Goshawk could carry four 112-pound bombs, two under each wing. Or it could carry a single 500-pound bomb beneath the fuselage. The fuselage bomb was stored in a special rack that swung down for release to prevent the bomb from hitting the propeller as it fell. A 50-gallon fuel tank could also be carried beneath the fuselage.

A later model of the aircraft was designed with a deep belly in the forward section of the fuselage that housed a retractable landing gear that the pilot operated with a hand crank. The first retractable landing gear on any single-seater, it served to add almost 20 miles per hour to the aircraft's performance.

Twenty-seven BFCs of this design were ordered.

They were assigned to the carrier *Ranger*. But because of problems with the landing gear, these planes had to be withdrawn from service after only a few months. Earlier Goshawks that had joined squadrons aboard the *Saratoga* enjoyed greater success, remaining in service until 1938.

Other Data (Model: BFC-2)
Type: Bomber-fighter
Wingspan: 31 ft., 6 in.
Length: 25 ft.
Power Plant: One 700-hp Wright Cyclone
Loaded Weight: 4,638 lb.
Maximum Speed: 205 mph

First ordered in 1934, the SBU remained in active service until outbreak of World War II in 1941.

VOUGHT SBU

In 1932, the Bureau of Aeronautics asked seven aircraft manufacturers to submit designs for a two-seat fighter. What was wanted was a plane with more power than the F8C Helldiver (page 14), yet one that would be able to perform satisfactorily at slow speeds for carrier landings.

The Chance Vought Corporation of East Hartford, Connecticut, on the basis of the design submitted by the company, received a contract to build a prototype on June 30, 1932.

Once the prototype became available, the Navy asked Chance Vought to modify the plane so it could serve as a scout bomber. This meant it would have to be able to drop bombs and also carry out information-gathering missions.

Engineers boosted the aircraft's fuel capacity and gave it stronger and larger wings. Bomb-carrying racks were installed. The plane was delivered to the Navy in June, 1934.

A fabric-covered biplane of metal construction, the SBU was powered by a Pratt & Whitney Twin Wasp Junior that delivered 700 hp. The aircraft cruised at a speed of 122 mph and was capable of 205 mph at 8,900 feet. It had a range of 548 miles.

The Navy ordered 84 SBU-1s in January, 1935. These were armed with two .30-caliber Browning machine guns, a forward-firing gun in the front cockpit, and a moveable gun in the rear cockpit.

Later, the Navy ordered a second batch of 40 SBUs. In these, the engine was upgraded and the plane's designation changed to SBU-2.

In total, the Navy purchased 126 SBUs. They served the fleet and naval reservists until shortly before the outbreak of World War II in 1941.

Other Data (Model: SBU-1)
Wingspan: 33 ft., 3 in.
Length: 27 ft., 10 in.
Power Plant: One 700-hp Pratt & Whitney Wasp
   Junior
Loaded Weight: 5,520 lb.
Maximum Speed: 205 mph at 8,900 ft.

Vought SBU was first planned as a two-seat fighter, but was then changed to a scout bomber.

VOUGHT SB2U VINDICATOR

A two-seat, low-wing monoplane with a retractable undercarriage, the SB2U Vindicator was one of the first of a new generation of Navy single-engine bombers of the late 1930s. Its presence signaled the end of the biplane era.

In October, 1934, when the Navy ordered a prototype fitting the Vindicator's description from Vought, the plane's monoplane design was seriously questioned. In fact, the Navy asked Vought to build a second prototype in a biplane format. But when the two prototypes were tested in April, 1935, the superiority of the monoplane was quickly established.

The Navy ordered 54 SB2U-1s in October, 1936. Work on the biplane version of the plane was halted. Delivery of these planes began late in December, 1937. They had the distinction of being the first carrier-based aircraft whose wings could be hydraulically folded when storing the plane aboard ship.

The SB2U was also exported. A large order went to the French government in 1938, only to be destroyed or captured by the Germans.

Fifty SB2Us were sent to Great Britain in 1941. These served with the Royal Navy as the Chesapeake 1. The British intended to assign the planes to duty aboard small escort carriers, but this wasn't possible because of the Vindicator's long takeoff

A low-wing monoplane with retractable landing gear, the SB2U Vindicator signaled the beginning of a new era in Navy bombers.

During early development stages, the SB2U was tested as a seaplane.

run. The plane was limited to shore-based assignments.

Vought built a total of 170 Vindicators for the Navy. They served as scout bombers and dive bombers aboard the *Lexington, Saratoga, Ranger,* and *Wasp.*

Many SB2Us were flown by Marine squadrons assigned to these ships. The plane was not known for its ruggedness. Indeed, to their Marine crews, the SB2U was sometimes referred to as, not the Vindicator, but the "Vibrator."

The Vindicator saw action against Japanese forces during the Battle of Midway in 1942. But soon after, the aircraft was withdrawn from service to be replaced by more modern types.

Other Data (Model: SB2U-3)
Wingspan: 42 ft.
Length: 34 ft.
Power Plant: One 825-hp Pratt & Whitney Twin Wasp Junior
Loaded Weight: 9,421 lb.
Maximum Special: 243 mph at 9,500 ft.

PB2Y's enormous hull offered a kitchen and sleeping accommodations for its nine-man crew.

CONSOLIDATED PB2Y CORONADO

Within only a few months after the first flight of the PBY Catalina (page 22), the Navy began making plans for a much bigger flying boat with better performance qualities. The result was the XPB2Y-1, also designed and built by Consolidated Aircraft Corporation. Later named the Coronado, the aircraft first flew on December 17, 1937.

The Coronado was powered by four Pratt & Whitney 1,200-hp engines (as compared to two engines for the Catalina). The aircraft was capable of speeds up to 223 mph and it had a cruising range of 2,300 miles. (While the PBY Catalina had greater range, its cruising speed was much less.)

The Coronado was the first U.S. military aircraft to be equipped with nose and tail gun turrets. In total, the aircraft was fitted with eight .50-caliber machine guns, making it a deadly fighter.

The Coronado could carry up to four 1,000-pound bombs beneath its giant wings, and as many as eight 1,000-pound bombs within its bomb bay.

The plane's enormous hull offered sleeping arrangments for its nine-man crew. There was a kitchen, too.

The Coronado might have gone into service earlier had the Navy had the funds to purchase the big plane. But what money the Navy did have for flying boats went to buy Catalinas, which cost only about one-third as much.

The Navy ordered six Coronados on March 31, 1939. The first of these was test-flown on December 31, 1940.

Because it was so expensive, the Coronado never achieved the success of the Catalina. It was withdrawn from active service in 1945, the year that World War II ended. By that time, many of the planes had been converted for use as transports.

The last of the Navy's seaplanes was phased out of service in the mid-1960s. "Helicopters are what did them in," says one observer. "Helicopters could land and take off from any flat surface, not just water. They cost less than seaplanes and didn't require as much maintenance.

"And they could do just about everything a seaplane could do. Once the helicopter became available, seaplanes just weren't needed anymore."

Other Data (Model: PB2Y-3)
Wingspan: 115 ft.
Length: 79 ft., 3 in.
Power Plant: Four 1,200-hp Pratt & Whitney Twin
    Wasp radial-piston engines
Loaded Weight: 68,000 lb.
Maximum Speed: 223 mph

First flown in 1937, PB2Y Coronados remained in service until end of World War II in 1945.

NORTHROP BT

John K. Northrop, well known as an airplane designer, formed his own company, the Northrop Aircraft Corporation, in 1929. He then began producing all-metal aircraft with advanced structural features. His output included the A-17 attack bomber, ordered by the Army Air Corps.

Using his experience in the development of the A-17 and other planes, Northrop, in 1934, designed a low-wing, all-metal scout/dive bomber for the Navy. Designated the BT-1, the plane was first flown during August of 1935.

The BT-1 was powered by an 825-hp Pratt & Whitney Twin Wasp Junior engine. It cruised at 192 mph and could attain a maximum speed of 222 mph. Northrop's plane had a range of 1,150 miles. It normally carried a 1,000-pound bomb.

Fifty-four BT-1s were ordered by the Navy. Deliveries began in 1938. The planes were assigned to

The two-seat, carrier-based Northrop BT had the range and ruggedness to serve as both a scout plane and dive bomber.

The BT could carry a 1,000-pound bomb. It was armed with both a .50-caliber and .30-caliber machine gun.

squadrons aboard the *Enterprise* and *Yorktown.* By the time of the Japanese attack on Pearl Harbor in December, 1941, the BT-1 was considered obsolete and had been withdrawn from service.

But there's more to the BT story. Northrop's designers and engineers continued to work to improve the plane, developing a completely retractable landing gear. (In the BT-1, the landing gear could be retracted only part of the way.) The aircraft's engine was upgraded and the shape of its tail modified, becoming slimmer.

By this time, the Northrop company had become part of the Douglas Aircraft Corporation. When the improved version of the BT went into production, the "T," which had stood for Northrop, was dropped in favor of "D" for Douglas. The aircraft became the SBD Dauntless (page 38), one of the most successful dive bombers of all time.

Other Data (Model: BT-1)
Wingspan: 41 ft., 6 in.
Length: 31 ft., 8 in.
Power Plant: One 825-hp Pratt & Whitney Twin
    Wasp Junior
Loaded Weight: 7,197 lb.
Maximum Speed: 222 mph at 9,500 ft.

A low-wing monoplane, the TBD Devastator had a cruising range of 435 miles, a maximum speed of 206 mph.

DOUGLAS TBD DEVASTATOR

The first torpedo bomber of monoplane design, the TBD Devastator was assigned to active duty with the fleet in 1937. When World War II broke out in December, 1941, Devastator squadrons were serving aboard the carriers *Lexington, Saratoga,* and *Enterprise.*

The aircraft had a crew of three—a pilot, radio operator/gunner, and a navigator/bombardier. A special window beneath the pilot's position enabled the bombardier, lying on his belly, to use a bombsight in launching the torpedo or dropping bombs.

While the rugged Devastator scored some modest successes in the early stages of World War II, the five-year-old aircraft was clearly overmatched at the Battle of Midway, one of the most famous naval engagements of all time. At Midway, squadrons of TBDs from the *Enterprise, Hornet,* and *Yorktown* faced a major part of the Japanese navy, including four aircraft carriers. The goal of the enemy task force was to destroy American naval installations on Midway Island.

The TBDs drifted in toward the Japanese vessels in three waves. To properly launch their torpedos, the TBDs had to keep the air speed to below 100 mph, and they had to approach within fifty or so feet of water. Coming in slow and low, the TBDs were exposed to murderous fire from

A photograph taken early in World War II shows TBD Devastators stored on flight deck of carrier *Enterprise*.

antiaircraft guns aboard the Japanese carriers and the ships meant to protect them. Japanese firepower also included the swift and highly maneuverable Japanese Zero fighter.

Most of the attacking TBDs were destroyed. One squadron lost all fifteen of its planes, and only one pilot survived.

But the TBDs' mission was not in vain. They drew the Zeros to low altitudes, and when American dive bombers—SBD Dauntlesses—attacked the Japanese carriers, they encountered almost no fighter opposition. The dive bombers quickly set off fires and explosions.

In total, the Japanese lost four carriers, a heavy cruiser, and 322 aircraft at Midway, losses from which they never really recovered. American losses included a carrier, a destroyer, and 150 aircraft.

After what had happened to the SBD Devastators at Midway, some observers said that the era of the torpedo bomber was over. Not at all. It was simply that the Devastator itself had become obsolete.

The surviving TBDs served briefly aboard the *Wasp* and *Ranger*, then were retired to shore bases. The role of the torpedo bomber was taken over by the Grumman TBF Avenger.

Other Data (Model: TBD-1)
Wingspan: 50 ft.
Length: 35 ft.
Power Plant: One 900-hp Pratt & Whitney
   Twin Wasp
Loaded Weight: 10,194 lb.
Maximum Speed: 206 mph at 8,000 ft.

A two-seat, midwing aircraft, the SB2A Buccaneer could carry a bombload of up to 1,000 pounds.

BREWSTER SB2A BUCCANEER

A plane that was meant to serve as either a land-based or carrier-based scout bomber, the two-seat Brewster Buccaneer was one of the less successful planes of its type in terms of both power and speed. The aircraft came into use during the late 1930s and early 1940s.

It was one of the most heavily armed aircraft of its time, however. It carried two .30-caliber guns, a turret just behind the wing, two in the forward section of the fuselage, and two others in each of the wings.

The Buccaneer was similar in design to a scout bomber the Brewster Aeronautical Corporation had developed for the Navy in 1934. The midwing Buccaneer was much bigger than the earlier aircraft, however. It carried its bombs within the fuselage, whereas most aircraft of the time carried them beneath the fuselage or wings.

The prototype of the aircraft that was to become the Buccaneer made its first flight on June 17, 1941. Not only was the aircraft produced for the Navy, but also for the British and Dutch air forces. The British used the Buccaneer as a land-based aircraft. They named it the Bermuda.

Hitler's armies were on the march in Europe at this time. In three months during 1940, six countries fell before the German onslaught—Denmark, Norway, Belgium, the Netherlands, Luxembourg, and France. The U.S. Navy took over the Buccaneers that had been ordered by the Dutch government.

The Buccaneer did not perform as well as other scout bombers that became available during the early stages of World War II. As a result, the aircraft was used chiefly as a trainer and utility plane. Despite its availability in the frantic early months of the war, there are no records to show that any Buccaneer was ever involved in combat.

Other Data (Model: SB2A-2)
Wingspan: 47 ft.
Length: 39 ft., 2 in.
Power Plant: One 1,700-hp Wright Cyclone
Loaded Weight: 14,289
Maximum Speed: 274 mph at 12,000 ft.

Although a total of 771 SB2As were built, none ever saw combat duty in World War II.

DOUGLAS SBD DAUNTLESS

During World War II, Navy pilots perfected the art of dive bombing. It took skill and daring on the part of the pilot, plus the ability to withstand the physical rigors of the dive itself. It also required a very rugged airplane.

Normally, warships were very elusive targets, able to turn, zigzag, or take other evasive action when under attack. But by diving down on the ship, and adjusting for the target's movement dur-ing the dive, it was possible to achieve a direct hit.

The dive bomber pilot would approach the target at high speed, taking advantage of cloud cover or, whenever possible, diving out of the sun. This made it difficult for defending antiaircraft gunners.

Dive bomber pilots liked to point out, "When we say dive, we mean straight down." A true vertical dive was considered ideal. Not only was it meant to assure accuracy, it had a defensive purpose. By rolling the plane in one direction or another during the dive, the pilot could avoid giving

No Navy aircraft had a finer record during World War II than the SBD Dauntless.

away the direction in which he was going to pull out. It was during the pullout that the dive bomber was the most vulnerable to antiaircraft fire.

Sometimes dive-bomber action was coordinated with a torpedo bomber attack. The dive bombers would go in first to disable the target. Then the torpedo bombers would finish it off. As one observer put it, "If you want to let in air, you use bombs. If you want to let in water, you use torpedoes."

At the time of Japan's attack on Pearl Harbor in December, 1941, the Navy's principal carrier-based dive bomber was the Douglas SBD Dauntless. A highly dependable aircraft that was well liked by its pilots, the Dauntless has been ranked as one of the most successful weapons of World War II.

The Dauntless design was based on that of the Northrop BT (page 32), although there were important engine and structural changes. The Dauntless was built to carry a 1,600-pound bomb in a rack under the fuselage, plus two 100-pound bombs on wing mounts. When used as a scout plane, the aircraft carried droppable fuel tanks on the wing mounts. The Dauntless had a range of 1,100 miles.

The first batch of SBDs was accepted by the Navy during February, 1939. In the years that followed, there were several model changes, these reflecting the lessons that were being learned in combat.

For example, fuel capacity was increased and

SBDs get set to make a second bombing run on a burning Japanese ship.

armor plate was added for the protection of the two-man crew. A more powerful engine, a Wright Cyclone that delivered 1,000 hp, was another modification.

39

Crew members of the carrier *Lexington* examine SBDs after their return from a World War II strike mission.

Planes with these modifications were dubbed SBD-2s and SBD-3s. By December, 1941, such aircraft had been assigned to the *Lexington, Enterprise, Yorktown,* and *Saratoga.* The next year, SBDs were delivered to additional Navy squadrons as well as many Marine squadrons.

The SBDs were star performers in virtually every naval engagement of the Pacific theater of operations. They played a major role in the battles of the Coral Sea and Midway. At Midway, they screamed out of the sky to sink four Japanese aircraft carriers. They helped to blunt the might of the Japanese Navy during the bitter struggle to regain control of the Solomon Islands. They provided air support for the Army during the invasion of the Philippine island of Luzon. They managed to give a good account of themselves during the Battle of the Philippine Sea, although they were all but obsolete by that time.

In total, 5,321 SBDs were supplied to the Navy. The SBD-5, produced in a new Douglas factory at Tulsa, Oklahoma, was the most-ordered version of the plane. This differed from earlier models by having a still more powerful engine, a 1,200-hp Wright

Cyclone, and more storage capacity for ammunition.

Late in 1944, the Navy began scaling down the number of SBDs it was ordering. A newer, more-sophisticated dive bomber, the SB2C Helldiver, had become available by that time. But not the Helldiver or any other dive bomber in naval aviation history was the equal of the Dauntless.

Other Data (Model: SBD-5)
Wingspan: 41 ft., 6¼ in.
Length: 33 ft.
Power Plant: One 1,200-hp Wright Cyclone
Loaded Weight: 10,855 lb.
Maximum Speed: 245 mph at 15,800 ft.

The Dauntless was flown into combat more than any other carrier-based bomber. A total of 5,991 were built.

Curtiss SB2C Helldivers from the *Ticonderoga* return to the carrier following the last air strike against Japan.

CURTISS SB2C HELLDIVER

The last and most famous of the Helldivers, the SB2C of the early 1940s, replaced the SBD Dauntless as the Navy's frontline carrier dive bomber. More SB2Cs were produced than any other dive bomber; a total of 6,649 was built.

First ordered on May 15, 1939, while the earlier Helldiver (page 20) was still in production, the new plane was a low-wing, two-seat monoplane. It first flew on December 18, 1940. Once a large order had been approved by the Navy, Curtiss built a new plant in Columbus, Ohio, to manufacture the aircraft.

The first SB2C-1s did not enter service until December, 1942, and another year went by before the aircraft was considered fully operational. Part of the delay was caused by the construction of the new factory. But there were other problems with the plane. It did not handle well. Pilots called it "The Beast" because it was so balky.

It also had a tendency to shed its wings during steep dives, hardly a good characteristic for a dive bomber. Restrictions were placed in the aircraft, and as a result it was never possible for the Helldiver to dive as steeply as the Dauntless could. In addition, the Helldiver's tail wheel had a habit of collapsing under great pressure.

There were good points about the Helldiver, however. It could carry a bigger load of bombs for a longer distance than any other dive bomber. The outer panels of the wings folded upward for carrier stowage. (The Dauntless did not have this capability.) Both crew positions were protected by armor plate.

The Helldiver first saw action against the Japanese on November 11, 1943, when a squadron of SB2Cs from the carrier *Bunker Hill* attacked harbor installations at Rabaul, New Guinea.

The aircraft earned its greatest praise at the Battle of Leyte Gulf (in the Philippine Islands), the last major sea battle of World War II (indeed, the last major sea battle in history). At Leyte Gulf, Helldivers attacked the *Yamato* and *Musashi*, at 70,000 tons, the biggest battleships ever built, and thought to be unsinkable. The Helldivers sent the *Musashi* to the bottom. While the *Yamato* escaped, it, too, was later destroyed by American dive bombers and torpedo bombers.

By the end of 1944, Helldivers had replaced the Dauntless in all carrier squadrons. Some SB2Cs served with the Naval Reserve in the years after World War II.

Other Data (Model: SB2C-4)
Wingspan: 49 ft., 9 in.
Length: 36 ft.
Power Plant: One 1,900-hp Wright Cyclone
Loaded Weight: 16,616 lb.
Maximum Speed: 295 mph at 16,700 ft.

Folding wings were one of the advantages that the Curtiss SB2C Helldiver had over the Douglas SBD Dauntless.

GRUMMAN TBF AVENGER

The World War II torpedo bomber had a three-fold mission: to launch torpedoes, drop bombs, and scout. No plane performed these jobs better than Grumman's TBF Avenger.

When the Japanese attacked Pearl Harbor on December 7, 1941, they provided a casebook demonstration in the use of carrier-based torpedo bombers. The first wave of attackers consisted of forty Nakajima B5N Kate torpedo bombers. They were followed by fifty Kates armed with bombs.

The Japanese wrought enormous destruction at Pearl Harbor, sinking four battleships and heavily damaging many other vessels. More than 2,400 Americans were killed. Japanese losses were relatively light.

In the months before the Pearl Harbor attack, the Navy rushed to get the Grumman TBF Avenger in service. It took shape as a chunky midwing airplane with a transparent covering over the canopy. It was to be the first aircraft of its type capable of carrying a 2,000-pound torpedo, or bombs of an equivalent weight, in an internal weapons bay.

The plane carried a crew of three—a pilot, bombardier, and a radio operator/gunner.

The first flight of the Avenger prototype took place on August 1, 1941. Deliveries of the first production models began the next year.

The Battle of Midway was a disaster for the

The rugged TBF Avenger was the Navy's most successful torpedo bomber of World War II.

Douglas TBD Devastator, the torpedo bomber the Avenger was meant to replace. Midway was also a catastrophe for the Avenger. Of six Avengers that saw action at Midway, only one surivived.

The Devastator's problem was that the plane had become obsolete. The Avengers at Midway suffered because their crews were inexperienced. They had been introduced to the aircraft only four weeks before at the Norfolk Naval Air Station.

By the summer of 1942, Grumman TBFs had replaced Douglas TBDs in every squadron, becoming the standard torpedo plane of the fleet. The aircraft built an outstanding record in the years that followed. In the Pacific theater, Avengers took part in the Battle of the Eastern Solomons during August, 1942, the Gilbert Islands later the following year, the Marshall Islands early in 1944, and the Battle of the Philippine Sea in June, 1944.

The Avenger was an extremely powerful plane, its Wright Cyclone engine delivering 1,700 hp. This power made it possible for the Avenger to get off a carrier deck in less than 650 feet. As a result, the aircraft was able to operate from the flight decks built on merchant ships that had been converted to escort carriers.

These vessels were vital in maintaining anti-

TBF Avengers on antisubmarine patrol pass the destroyer John A. Bole.

submarine patrols with attack convoys, providing support for amphibious landings, and resupplying the bigger attack carriers after battle losses. The Avenger played an important role in all of these operations.

At first, Grumman produced the Avenger side-by-side with the F6F Hellcat, a renowned Navy fighter. The demand for Avengers soon outgrew Grumman's ability to supply both that plane and the Wildcat. A second source was established, the Eastern Aircraft Division of General Motors. Avengers began flowing from the company's Trenton, New Jersey, plant in September, 1942.

The Avenger's rear turret housed a radio operator/ gunner. Crew also included the pilot and bombardier.

A total of 8,852 Avengers were built. No other naval aircraft was produced in such quantity.

In the later stages of the war, Avengers that had been supplied to Britain's Royal Air Navy supported American operations in the Pacific. Avengers from such British carriers as the *Formidable*, *Illustrious*, and *Victorious* bombed Japanese oil refineries in the East Indies and conducted raids on the island of Formosa and the Japanese home islands, including Tokyo itself.

Radar-equipped Avengers worked with the Navy's first experimental night fighters in the Pacific. Other versions were fitted with submarine radar or aerial cameras.

When World War II ended in 1945, Avenger production ceased. But the plane's career continued. Carrying advanced radar equipment, Avengers were used in searching for and locating deep-diving nuclear submarines. Other Avengers were fitted with special electronic equipment meant to counter enemy radar systems. Still other TBFs were used to tow targets in gunnery practice or in COD (Carrier On-board Delivery) operations. These versions of the plane continued to fly well into the 1950s.

Right: Despite the damage it sustained, this World War II TBF Avenger flew 100 miles back to its carrier group. Although it crash-landed in the water, all crew members were rescued.

Other Data (Model: TBF-1)
Wingspan: 54 ft., 2 in.
Length: 40 ft.
Power Plant: One 1,700-hp Wright Cyclone
Loaded Weight: 15,905 lb.
Maximum Speed: 271 mph at 12,000 ft.

In a photograph taken in **1942**, **TBF Avengers** cruise in formation.

First flown in 1944, the AM Mauler was biggest and heaviest aircraft ever built for operation from a carrier.

MARTIN AM MAULER

In 1944, with the end of World War II in sight, the Navy began seeking a new type of airplane. It was to be bigger and more powerful than any carrier-based aircraft then available. It was to combine the missions of both the torpedo bomber and the scout/dive bomber. It was to be designated the Navy's first attack plane.

The plane's mission would be to carry out the primary goal of the carrier strike force: to deliver the bombload against the enemy on the ground.

The Navy ordered two prototypes from the Martin Aircraft Company on May 31, 1944, and another from Douglas Aircraft on July 21 of that year. The Martin plane first flew on August 26, 1944.

Unlike the Avenger and Dauntless or other highly regarded planes of the time, the Mauler was designed as a single-seater. The weight saved was used for the aircraft's bombload.

Bomb-carrying was what the Martin aircraft did best. Racks were mounted at fifteen points beneath the wings and fuselage for bombs, torpedoes, or rockets—anything. In total, the Mauler could carry about 4,500 pounds of ordnance, more than twice that of the Dauntless.

Powered by a 2,975-hp Wright Cyclone engine, the Mauler was powerfully armed, carrying four 20-mm cannons in the wings. Its cruising speed was 200 mph, and its top speed was in excess of 350 mph.

The Navy ordered 750 AMs early in 1945. The

first of these was delivered to the fleet on March 1, 1948.

During this period, the aircraft was still being test-flown, as was the Douglas prototype. The Navy eventually decided it wanted only one attack plane, and chose the model that had been designed by Douglas. This aircraft came to be known as the AD-1 Skyraider (page 50).

Mauler production was halted in October, 1949. Of the 750 aircraft that had been ordered, only 151 were built, including the prototypes.

During 1950, the Maulers that had managed to get assigned to active duty were withdrawn to allow carrier squadrons to begin flying AD-1 Skyraiders. The Maulers ended up with units of the U.S. Naval Reserve.

Other Data (Model: AM-1)
Wingspan: 50 ft.
Length: 41 ft., 2 in.
Power Plant: One 2,975-hp Wright
    Cyclone
Loaded Weight: 23,386 lb.
Maximum Speed: 367 mph at 11,600 ft.

Racks mounted beneath the wings and fuselage enabled the Mauler to carry a variety of bombs, torpedoes, or rockets.

Skyraiders from the carrier *Kitty Hawk* fly in tight formation.

DOUGLAS AD-1 SKYRAIDER

Developed during the final stages of World War II, the AD-1 Skyraider, a piston-engine plane, arrived too late to see action in that conflict. But it proved to be one of the most valuable of all weapons available to American forces during the Korean War and Vietnam War. Indeed, during the Korean campaign, where the plane was frequently used to back up ground forces, one Navy official described the Skyraider as the "best and most effective close-support aircraft in the world."

The Skyraider was first ordered by the Navy on July 6, 1944. Specifications called for an aircraft capable of carrying any type of ordnance—bombs or torpedoes, mines or depth charges, rockets or missiles. It also had to have the capability of any aircraft of its type that had gone before.

Other aircraft with these specifications were ordered from competing manufacturers. The Douglas Skyraider, an all-metal, low-wing monoplane, proved clearly the best.

The first production aircraft were delivered to the Navy in June, 1945. World War II ended with the surrender of Japan on August 14, 1945, before any Skyraider saw active duty. A total of 548 aircraft had been ordered by the Navy, but this order was cut drastically when the war ended.

The Skyraider was scheduled for retirement in the late 1940s and early 1950s. But in 1950, the Korean War broke out. Within three days after the United States had agreed to the support of the United Nations resolution backing the Republic of Korea in resisting invasion from the north, Skyraiders from the carrier *Valley Forge* attacked targets north of Seoul, the capital. From that time on until the war ended in 1953, the Skyraider was seldom absent from Korean skies.

Production of the Skyraider, which had been resumed during the Korean conflict, ceased for good in 1957. Many different versions of the aircraft were produced besides the single-seat attack model. It also served as a cargo or personnel carrier, an ambulance plane, and a trainer. A total of 3,180 Skyraiders were built.

When the last attack version of the piston-engine Skyraider returned on April 6, 1968, it marked the end of an era. Attack aircraft of the future would be jets.

Other Data (Model: AD-2)
Wingspan: 50 ft.
Length: 38 ft., 2 in.
Power Plant: One 2,700-hp Wright Cyclone
Loaded Weight: 18,263 lb.
Maximum Speed: 321 mph at 18,300 ft.

Skyraiders are massed on the deck of the carrier *Intrepid* as the vessel steams in the South China Sea in support of Seventh Fleet operations in Vietnam.

51

McDONNELL-DOUGLAS A-4 SKYHAWK

Sometimes called "Heinemann's Hotrod" after its designer, Ed Heinemann, the Skyhawk was the Navy's chief weapon during the Vietnam War. A single-seat attack bomber, the Skyhawk supported United Nations troops in offensive operations against guerrillas in South Vietnam. It also struck selected ground targets in the North. In both roles, the plane was widely hailed for its pinpoint accuracy.

In developing the Skyhawk, which was intended as a jet-powered successor to the AD-1 Skyraider (page 50), Heinemann sought a plane that would be simpler, lighter in weight, and inexpensive.

The Skyhawk's turbojet engine was placed in the rear of the fuselage behind the cockpit. Electronic gear was housed in the nose section.

The Skyhawk was such a compact aircraft that it did not need folding wings for shipboard storage. By eliminating this feature, Heinemann was able to achieve wings that were much lighter.

A single-seat attack bomber, the A-4 Skyhawk could carry a wide range of weapons.

A-4 Skyhawk (right) hooks up with an A-7 Corsair II for in-flight refueling.

The first of two Skyhawk prototypes was ready for testing in June, 1954. Deliveries to fleet squadrons began in October, 1956.

The A-4 Skyhawk went into action in Vietnam during the summer of 1964. North Vietnamese torpedo boats had attacked two American destroyers. Skyhawks joined other aircraft in retaliating, raiding the torpedo-boat bases.

For most of the next three years, the A-4 bombed North Vietnam. The plane won high praise for the amount and variety of weaponry that it could handle. This included some 8,200 pounds of bombs, missiles, or rockets at five different placement points beneath the wings and fuselage. Fuel tanks or gun pods could also be mounted at any one of these five stations.

In mid-August, 1965, two A-4s became the first Navy aircraft to be brought down by surface-to-air

missiles. One of the Skyhawks exploded and crashed, while the other, badly damaged, managed to limp back to the carrier *Midway*.

More than 3,000 Skyhawks were produced. The plane was used by several foreign nations, including Argentina, Australia, New Zealand, and Israel.

The Navy took delivery of its last Skyhawks in 1979. By that time, the plane had been in continuous production for 23 years. No other military plane had a longer production run.

Other Data (Model: A-4M)
Wingspan: 27 ft., 6 in.
Length: 40 ft., 3¾ in.
Power Plant: One 11,200-lb.-thrust Pratt &
    Whitney turbojet
Loaded Weight: 24,500 lbs.
Maximum Spede: 670 mph at sea level

An A-6 Intruder is readied for launching on the flight deck of the aircraft carrier *Saratoga*.

GRUMMAN A-6 INTRUDER

Out of the Navy's participation in the Korean War, a need developed for a carrier-based attack plane that could swoop in on its target at about treetop level to elude enemy radar while flying at the speed of sound. The plane also had to be capable of finding and hitting small targets in the worst of weather, night or day.

Grumman's A-6 Intruder was developed to fill these needs. The prototype first flew on April 9, 1960. The first deliveries to fleet squadrons began three years later, in 1963.

Intruders from the carrier *Independence* began operating in support of American forces in Vietnam in 1965. Navy Intruders flew from the decks of

carriers of the seventh fleet. Marine Corps Intruder squadrons were shore-based. The plane continued to be active in Vietnam until the war ended.

Later models of the Intruder were equipped with TRAM—Target Recognition Attack Multisensor. This electronic system provides an image of those targets that cannot be detected by radar. TRAM combined with a laser system to guide the weapon to its target.

Another version of the Intruder was developed as an ECM—Electronic Countermeasure—aircraft. Modern antiaircraft systems rely on radar for tracking the target and guiding the weapon to the target. The Intruder was fitted out with more than thirty different antennas to be used in detecting, locating, and jamming enemy radar transmissions.

This plane was designated the EA-6A. (The "E" stands for electronic.)

The plane was later redesigned to carry a crew of four. Two additional crewmen operated the aircraft's electronic gear. This plane was designated the EA-6B and named the Prowler. Today, EA-6B Prowlers serve aboard every Navy aircraft carrier.

Other Data (Model: A-6E)
Wingspan: 53 ft.
Length: 54 ft., 7 in.
Power Plant: Two Pratt & Whitney turbojets delivering 18,600 lbs. total thrust
Loaded Weight: 60,400 lbs.
Maximum Speed: 648 mph at sea level

A plane captain aboard the carrier *Forrestal* checks the cockpit of an A-6 Intruder.

LTV A-7 CORSAIR II

In mid-1963, the Navy called upon several aircraft manufacturers to submit designs for a single-seat, single-engine, carrier-based attack bomber. The new aircraft was needed to replace the A-4 Skyhawk (page 52).

LTV Aerospace and Defense Company of Dallas, Texas, won the competition. The company's designers based their proposal, at least in part, on the F-8 Crusader, the highly regarded fighter of the late 1950s and early 1960s. LTV, known as the Vought Company at the time, had built the F-8 in large numbers for the Navy.

The A-7's nickname, Corsair II, honored another famous Navy fighter, the World War II F4U Corsair, which had also been built by Vought.

Pilots who flew the A-7 had their own name for the plane, however. They called it the "SLUF," an acronym for Short Little Ugly Fellow. Indeed, the Corsair II was anything but sleek and handsome. Yet it proved to be a very effective plane in several different roles.

The A-7 had a short, stumpy body and wings with little sweepback. The plane looked like it was built to carry a big load—and it was. The A-7 had eight stations on the fuselage sides and beneath

An A-7 Corsair II circles the carrier *Saratoga* before making its landing approach.

the wings for storing munitions. These stations could accommodate virtually every type of weapon in the Navy's arsenal. The A-7 could carry up to 15,000 pounds of armament.

The first A-7 flew on September 27, 1965. Deliveries to Navy squadrons began in September and October of the following year.

During the war in Vietnam, the A-7 was equipped with sophisticated radar and navigation equipment that enabled the aircraft to bomb accurately day or night, no matter what the weather.

Tactical bombing wasn't the plane's only assignment. A-7s were also used in search and rescue missions, for aerial minelaying, target recognition, and as tankers for in-flight refueling.

By the end of the Vietnam conflict, the A-7 had flown more than 6,000 combat missions. Only four aircraft were lost to enemy fire. No other Navy plane had a better record.

Other Data (Model: A-7E)
Wingspan: 38 ft., 9 in.
Length: 46 ft., 1½ in.
Power Plant: One 14,250-lb.-thrust Allison
    turbofan
Loaded Weight: 42,000 lbs.
Maximum Speed: 700 mph at sea level

Right: Carrier *Saratoga*'s elevator totes a pair of A-7s from flight deck to hangar deck for storage.

Part of a squadron of A-7s on the flight deck of the carrier *America*.

McDONNELL-DOUGLAS HARRIER II

A single-seat, attack aircraft, the Harrier II has the unique ability of being able to take off and land in a space no bigger than a tennis court. Under wartime conditions, this could mean the Harrier could operate not merely from a carrier flight deck, but also from the damaged runway of an airfield, a short section of road, or a grassy strip near the field of battle.

A helicopter uses its big rotor blade to achieve lift. In the case of the Harrier II, the aircraft captures energy from the exhaust of its Rolls Royce Pegasus turbofan engine, and then uses that energy to provide upward thrust.

The Harrier II has a one-piece wraparound windshield and swept-back wings. It is capable of a maximum speed of 720 mph at an altitude of 1,000 feet.

The aircraft can do things that are impossible for other aircraft. It can almost stop in the sky, or at least decelerate so quickly that other aircraft overshoot it. This quality, plus the Harrier's relatively small size, makes it a highly elusive opponent.

The Harrier II is armed with air-to-air Sidewinder missiles and two 25-mm cannons. It can also carry almost five tons of bombs and rockets or air-to-ground missiles.

The Harrier II was developed through an international cooperation project between the Mc-

From a typical forward site, Harrier can get to its target in ten minutes or less, or about one-third the time it takes a conventional aircraft.

With a weapons payload that includes Sidewinder heat-seeking missiles, plus its two 25-mm cannons, the Harrier is very good at defending itself.

Donnell-Douglas Company and Great Britain's Hawker-Siddeley Aviation Ltd. The aircraft is used by military forces of both nations.

The first Harriers began operating with the British Navy in 1970 and with American forces in 1971. The U.S. Marine Corps has obtained 336 Harriers for use in supporting ground operations.

Other Data (Model: AV-8B II)
Wingspan: 30 ft., 6 in.
Length: 46 ft., 4 in.
Power Plant: One 21,500-lb.-thrust Rolls Royce
  Pegasus turbofan
Loaded Weight: 21,150 lbs.
Maximum Speed: 720 mph at 1,000 ft.

F/A-18 Hornets prepare for launching during flight operations aboard carrier *Carl Vinson*.

McDONNELL-DOUGLAS F/A-18 HORNET

The Navy's newest airplane is unique. It represents a successful attempt to combine the qualities of a fighter and attack plane in one aircraft, thus its designation "F/A"—F for fighter, A for attack plane.

The Navy began taking delivery of the first Hornets early in the 1980s. Some observers have forecast that the plane will continue in service with the Navy for the rest of the century and even beyond.

A single-seat, twin-jet aircraft, the Hornet offers nine stations beneath the fuselage and wings where a variety of weapons or extra fuel tanks can be mounted. What the Hornet carries in the way of external equipment varies with the role it is assigned.

As a fighter plane, it carries air-to-air combat weapons. These include two radar-guided Sparrow missiles that are mounted at the lower edge of the fuselage and two heat-seeking Sidewinder missiles carried at the wing tips. A 20-mm cannon with 570 rounds of ammunition is carried in the nose.

As an attack aircraft, one meant for air-to-surface missions, the Hornet carries ground attack weapons. It retains the Sidewinder missiles and the cannon for self-defense. It also carries (in place of the Sparrow missiles) infrared and laser sensors that provide information for either dropping bombs or firing missiles.

The Hornet's top speed is 1,130 mph, almost twice the speed of sound. At 35,000 feet, it can accelerate from 530 mph to 1,060 mph in less than two minutes.

The Hornet also performs very well at less than

Wing-tip Sidewinder missiles are part of armament carried by F/A-18 Hornet.

the speed of sound. This is an asset in aerial combat where supersonic speeds are seldom necessary. During the Vietnam War, the supersonic pilot often ended up a prisoner because his engine gulped down so much fuel it eventually ran dry. Forced to eject, the pilot was captured.

Despite its many superior qualities, the Hornet is less than perfect. Its critics say that designing the plane to perform two different missions weakened its ability to fulfill either. The plane's range and endurance, vital factors, make the Hornet effective as a fighter.

One serious problem came to light in 1984. A design-failing was causing cracks in the plane's distinctive tail fins. Changes in the tail structure were ordered.

Despite the problems, by the mid-1980s, the Hornet had replaced the F-4 Phantom II, a fighter, and the A-7 Corsair, an attack plane, in many squadrons. The Navy and Marine Corps had ordered a total of 1,377 Hornets. The air forces of Canada and Australia were planning to fly them, too.

Other Data (Model: F-18A)
Wingspan: 37½ ft.
Length: 56 ft.
Power Plant: Two General Electric Turbofans
   delivering 32,000-lbs total thrust
Loaded Weight: 35,000 lbs.
Maximum Speed: Approximately 1,130 mph
   (Mach 1.8)

AIRCRAFT DESIGNATION SYSTEM

All naval aircraft (and Air Force aircraft, too) are given coded designations to indicate the mission and design number of each. The system in use today was adopted in 1962.

Here are the mission symbols:

Symbol	Mission
A	Attack
B	Bomber
C	Cargo/Transport
E	Special Electronics
F	Fighter
K	Tanker
O	Observation
P	Patrol
S	Antisubmarine
T	Trainer
U	Utility
X	Research

Thus, the plane designated A-7 is an attack aircraft, the seventh design in the series.

Two other symbols can be used to indicate aircraft type. They are:

H	Helicopter
V	VTOL or STOL

A plane designated AV-8 is an attack aircraft with VTOL (vertical takeoff and landing) capability. It is the eighth design in the series. SH-3 is an antisubmarine helicopter, the third design in the series.

An additional letter is sometimes used before the other letters and numbers. This prefix indicates a special status the aircraft may have. The six status prefix letters are:

Letter	Status
G	Permanently grounded
J	Special test, temporary
N	Special test, permanent
X	Experimental
Y	Prototype
Z	Planning

Before 1962, the designation system gave more information. It was usually made up of four units. The first unit, either one or two letters, indicated the function of the aircraft: PB stood for patrol bomber; SB for scout bomber and TB for torpedo bomber. The second unit was a number denoting the model.

The third unit, one letter, indicated the manufacturer of the aircraft; B stood for Boeing Aircraft Co; C for Curtiss Aeroplane & Motor Co., and F for Grumman Aircraft Corp.

In the case of F6F-3, the F stood for fighter; the 6 meant it was the sixth fighter of its type; the second F indicated the plane was manufactured by Grumman. The final -3 meant it was the third modification of the basic design.